The Ultimate

Air Fryer

Cookbook

Discover the Magic of Air Frying with these Flavorful Recipes

James S. Smith

TABLE OF CONTENTS

INTRODUCTION

In order to cook food that would normally be covered in oil, air fryers circulate hot air. A heating source placed close to the food emits heat into the air fryer's frying chamber, while a fan moves the heated air about.

With a small volume of hot air forced to pass from the heater surface and over the food, rather than idle air circulating as in a convection oven, the original Philips Airfryer delivered heat from all sides using radiant heat from a heating element just above the food and convection heat from a strong air stream flowing upward through the open bottom of the food chamber. The wind was directed over the food's bottom via a shaped guide. Rapid Air technology was the name given to the method.

Traditional frying techniques totally immerse food in heated oil, considerably above the boiling point of water, to trigger the Maillard reaction at temperatures between 140 and 165 °C (284 and 329 °F). The meal is covered in a small layer of oil in the air fryer, which circulates air heated to up to 200 °C (392 °F) to ignite the reaction.

The majority of air fryers allow for temperature and timer adjustments, which facilitate more exact cooking. Usually, cooking takes place in a basket that rests on a drip tray. Either manually or by the fryer mechanism, the basket needs to be stirred up from time to time. While air fryers and convection ovens both cook food in a similar manner, air fryers are typically smaller and produce less heat.

Once you learn how they operate, air fryers are quick and may be used to cook a variety of fresh items, including chicken, steak, pork chops, fish, and vegetables, as well as to thaw frozen goods. Because most meats are already so juicy, they don't need additional oil; simply season them with salt and your preferred herbs and spices.

Always use dry seasonings since less moisture yields crispier results. Wait until the last few minutes of cooking to baste meats with barbecue sauce or honey.

Foods with little to no fat or lean cuts of meat need oil to brown and crisp up. Before seasoning, lightly oil boneless chicken breasts and pork chops. Due to their higher smoke points, vegetable or canola oil is typically advised since they can withstand the high heat in an air fryer.

In addition, vegetables must be coated in oil before air frying. Use a little less salt than usual when you sprinkle them with salt before air frying because the flavorful, crunchy bits are packed with flavor. Broccoli florets, Brussels sprouts, and baby potato halves are all delicious when air-fried. They turn out so crunchy! Beets, butternut squash, and sweet potatoes all seem to get sweeter over time, while green beans and peppers grow quickly.

WHY ARE PEOPLE BUYING AIR FRYERS?

Because they are less expensive, use less oil than conventional fryers, and heat food quickly and uniformly, air fryers are very popular. These devices operate more quickly than a typical convection oven and are significantly healthier than deep fryers.

IS AIR FRYER BETTER THAN OVEN?

Both ovens and air fryers can reheat food, but air fryers come out on top in this contest. In addition to heating food more quickly than a traditional oven, air fryers also produce food that is evenly heated and wonderfully crispy, giving stale pizza, sloppy fries, and much more new life.

IS AIR FRIED FOOD HEALTHY?

Are Air-Fried Foods Healthier? Air frying is generally considered to be healthier than oil frying. It reduces calories by 70% to 80% and contains significantly less fat. This cooking method may help reduce some of the other negative impacts of oil frying.

ARE AIR FRYERS HARMFUL TO YOUR HEALTH?

Summary. Despite the possibility that air-frying is healthier than deep-frying, harmful chemicals are still present, albeit at lower concentrations. In addition, compared to deep frying, air frying takes longer and yields food with a somewhat different flavor and texture.

BREAKFAST RECIPES

AIR FRYER APPLE FRITTERS WITH BROWN BUTTER GLAZE

Prep time:10 minutes

Total time:20 minutes

Serving: 4

Ingredients

BROWN BUTTER GLAZE

- 1 cup Powdered Sugar
- ¼ cup Butter, (½ stick)
- ½ tsp Vanilla
- 1 tbsp Milk, if needed

APPLE FRITTERS

- 1 ½ cups All Purpose Flour
- ¼ cup Granulated Sugar
- 2 tsp Baking Powder
- ½ tsp Salt
- 1 ½ tsp Ground Cinnamon
- ⅓ cup Milk
- 1 tsp Vanilla
- 1 tbsp Lemon Juice, fresh
- 2 Eggs
- 2 large Apples peeled, cored and diced small
- Canola or Vegetable Oil, for brushing/spraying

Instructions

BROWN BUTTER GLAZE

In a smallish saucepan set over medium-high warmth, add the butter. The butter should keep melting until it begins to froth and turn brown. Remove from burner once browned and allow to cool slightly. The butter should have brown flecks and have a nutty aroma.

To a small bowl, add powdered sugar. While whisking, add the milk, vanilla, and brown butter. Place aside.

APPLE FRITTERS

Set the air fryer to a temperature of 400 phases Fahrenheit and wait 3 to 4 minutes for the inner basket to get nice and hot.

In the meantime, combine the cinnamon, salt, baking soda, and flour in a medium basin.

In the center, create a well and pour in the milk, vanilla, lemon juice, and eggs. After thoroughly combining, fold the apples in.

Carefully place a piece of parchment paper or an air fryer basket liner into the preheated air fryer's basket. To prevent edge overlap, I like to trim the parchment to fit the bottom. Apply oil sparingly on a brush or with an oil sprayer.

Onto the lined air fryer basket, pour around 14 cup of the batter. You might only be able to fit 2 fritters in your air fryer at once, depending on its size.

Using a pastry brush or oil sprayer, lightly coat the fritters' tops in oil. For 4-5 minutes or until the fritters are a deep golden brown, preheat the air fryer to 400 degrees. Reverse the fritters and continue.

Place the apple fritters on a cooling rack while they are still warm and drizzle with the brown butter glaze.Serve immediately and enjoy!

AIR FRYER BREAKFAST BURRITOS

Prep time:20 minutes

Total time:23 minutes

Serving: 8

Ingredients

- 1 pound breakfast sausage
- 1 bell pepper, chopped
- 12 eggs beaten together
- ½ teaspoon black pepper
- 1 teaspoon sea salt
- 8 flour tortillas burrito size
- 2 cups shredded colby jack cheese or use your favorite cheese

Instructions

In a big skillet, brown the sausage by crumbling it. Add chopped peppers and stir. Sausage should be drained of grease and placed on a dish covered with paper towels.

One tablespoon of butter should be softened in a sizable skillet. Add the eggs, salt, and pepper, and cook while continuously turning until the eggs are mostly set and no extended runny.

Add the cooked sausage, then turn off the heat.

A tortilla should have some of the egg and sausage mixture in the center, some cheese on top, the sides folded in, and it should be rolled up.

Set air fryer to 390 degrees before using.

Lightly mist burritos with olive oil spray.

As many burritos as will fit in the air fryer basket or Instant Pot Vortex trays should be placed there. Cook the burritos for 3 minutes at 390 degrees for the air fryer basket and 2 minutes in the Vortex, turning the trays halfway through. Cook burritos in the Vortex for three minutes if you want them extra dark or crispier.

Remove and serve right away, or let it cool just enough to wrap well and freeze for later.

AIR FRYER CINNAMON ROLLS

Prep time:2 minutes

Total time:10 minutes

Serving: 8

Ingredients

- 1 Can of Pillsbury Cinnamon Rolls 8-Count
- Coconut Oil Cooking Spray

Instructions

Spray coconut oil cooking spray to the Ninja Foodi or Air Fryer's basket.

Put the cinnamon rolls in the basket in a uniform distribution.

Set the icing aside.

The cinnamon rolls should be air-fried for 8 minutes at 360 degrees.

Check on them after 7 minutes to make sure they are frying properly because every air fryer heats differently.

Once finished, carefully remove and ice the top.Serve.

AIR FRYER BREAKFAST SAUSAGE

Prep time:10 minutes

Total time:12 minutes

Serving: 10

Ingredients

- 10 breakfast sausages

Instructions

Set the air fryer's temperature to 370 degrees F.

Place the breakfast sausages onto the air fryer tray once it is hot. To ensure that the sausages cook evenly, avoid packing the air fryer too full.

The sausages should be fully cooked through and crispy on the outside after 10 to 12 minutes of cooking. Halfway through, give the air fryer basket a gentle shake or use tongs to flip the sausages. The cook time may differ significantly depending on the thickness of the sausages, your preferred level of crispiness, and your air fryer..

AIR FRYER CHEESY GARLIC BREAD ROLLS

Prep time:5 minutes

Total time:10 minutes

Serving: 4

Ingredients

- 2 large sub rolls
- 1/4 cup butter, melted, unsalted
- 1 cup shredded mozzarella cheese
- 2-3 teaspoons minced garlic
- 1 teaspoon Italian seasoning

Instructions

The butter should first be melted in a basin before going into the microwave.

Add the mozzarella cheese, garlic powder, and Italian seasoning together.

Spread the mixture on top of the bread after cutting it into two pieces.

Place the bread in the basket of the air fryer.

Set the timer for 4 minutes and the temperature to 370 degrees F.

Plate, provide, and indulge!

TWO-INGREDIENT BANANA PANCAKES

Prep time:5 minutes

Total time:5 minutes

Serving: 1

Ingredients

- Vegetable oil, as needed
- 2 large eggs
- 1 ripe medium banana

Directions

Oil is added to a skillet that is already at medium heat.

In a blender, process the eggs and banana for 30 to 60 seconds, or until extremely smooth. Cook the banana mixture for one minute after pouring it into the hot skillet. For one more minute, flip and cook. Serve right away.

AIR FRYER FRENCH TOAST

Prep time:5 minutes

Total time:10 minutes

Serving: 4

Ingredients

- cooking spray
- 3 large eggs
- ½ cup milk
- 1 teaspoon vanilla extract
- ½ teaspoon cinnamon
- Pinch salt
- 8 slices brioche bread

Instructions

Set the air fryer to 375°F, line it with parchment paper, and, if necessary, spray it with cooking spray.

Whisk the eggs, milk, vanilla, cinnamon, and a dash of salt in a big shallow basin.

Each slice of bread should be dipped into the egg mixture, then turned over to coat the other side. As many pieces of the french toast sticks—roughly 8–12—that will fit in the air fryer at once should be placed there.

Cook for 5 to 6 minutes, or until the french toast is golden brown and fluffy.

If desired, drizzle the warm french toast sticks with maple syrup and dust with powdered sugar.

AIR FRYER CHERRY HOMEMADE POP-TARTS

Prep time:10 minutes

Total time:40 minutes

Serving:10

Ingredients

- All-purpose flour for dusting optional
- 14.1 ounce package of refrigerated pie crusts contains two pie crusts
- 10-12 tbsp cherry pie filling
- Water
- 1½ cups powdered sugar
- 2-3 tbsp whole milk
- 1 tbsp lemon juice ½ a lemon
- Sprinkles optional garnish

Instructions

Roll out the pie crusts to a thickness of 1/4 inch on a hard surface after lightly dusting it with all-purpose flour.

Even rectangles of 3 inches by 4 inches can be carved out of the dough using a knife or pizza cutter. If there is any extra dough, combine it and roll it out once more to make as many rectangles as you can.

12–1 Tablespoon of cherry pie filling should be placed in the center of each rectangle.

Each rectangle containing the filling should have the edges moistened with water using a pastry brush.

Place the empty rectangles on top of the cherry-filled rectangles, aligning the edges.

The edges of each pop tart should be sealed by applying pressure with the point of a fork.

Apply cooking spray to the tops of the pop tarts, and then cut 2-3 slits in the tops of each pop pie with a knife.

Cook for 7-8 minutes in the air fryer at 350 degrees Fahrenheit or until the edges are just beginning to brown. You'll need to work in several bunches.

Set the pop tarts aside to cool after they have finished baking.

While waiting, combine the whole milk, powdered sugar, and lemon juice in a medium bowl and whisk until combined.

Sprinkles are optional, but you can drizzle the glaze over the cooled pop tarts, plate them, and serve them cold.

JUICY AIR FRYER TURKEY BURGERS

Prep time:5 minutes

Total time:50 minutes

Serving:4

Ingredients

- 1 lb ground turkey 85/15
- ¼ cup unsweetened apple sauce
- ½ onion grated
- 1 Tablespoon ranch seasoning
- 2 teaspoon Worcestershire Sauce
- 1 teaspoon minced garlic
- ¼ cup plain breadcrumbs
- Salt and pepper to taste

Instructions

Onion, ground turkey, unsweetened apple sauce, ranch seasoning, Worchester sauce, minced garlic, breadcrumbs, salt, and pepper should all be combined. Use your hands to blend the ingredients. Form into 4 hamburger patties of the same size.

Then, to help them somewhat firm up, put your burgers in the refrigerator for about 30 minutes.

Run your air fryer at 360 degrees for roughly 3 minutes to reach the desired temperature. Make sure your Air fryer is empty before placing your burgers on it. Cook for 15 minutes at 360 degrees, flipping once. When your hamburgers register a temperature of 165 degrees Fahrenheit on a quick-read thermometer, they are done.

AIR FRYER LEMON COD

Prep time:10 minutes

Total time:25minutes

Serving:2

Ingredients

- 1 pound cod filets, fresh or frozen then thawed
- 1/4 teaspoon sea salt flakes
- 1/4 teaspoon fresh ground black pepper
- 2 tablespoons unsalted butter
- 1 teaspoon fresh dill
- 1 teaspoon fresh lemon zest
- 1 tablespoons fresh lemon juice
- 1 lemon sliced

Instructions

Aerator should be heated to 375 degrees.

After using a paper towel to pat the filets dry, season them with salt and pepper on both sides.

Melt the butter in a tiny, shallow bowl, then stir in the dill and zest. To blend, stir.

Prepare a parchment paper lining for the air fryer basket.

Place each filet in the air fryer basket with space between them after dipping it in the butter mixture and coating both sides.

Add some lemon juice and a slice of lemon to the top of each filet.

Cook for 15 minutes, or until an instant-read thermometer reads 145 degrees Fahrenheit inside the thickest section of the filet.

AIR FRYER CHICKEN WINGS

Prep time:20 minutes

Total time:45minutes

Serving:2

Ingredients

- Nonstick cookery spray, for the basket
- 2 pounds chicken branches, split at the joint and tips removed
- Kosher salt
- 4 tablespoons unsalted butter
- 1/2 cup hot flavoring, such as Frank's RedHot
- Ranch or blue cheese gravy, for serving

Directions

A 3.5-quart air fryer's basket should be sprayed with cooking spray before being placed away. Dry off the chicken wings with paper towels and liberally salt them. The wings should not touch as you place them in the fryer basket. After cooking the wings for 12 minutes at 360 degrees Fahrenheit, flip them over with tongs and continue cooking for another 12 minutes. The wings should cook for a further 6 minutes after being turned over, with the heat increased to 390 degrees F.

In the meantime, microwave the butter in a bowl that is microwave-safe for about a minute, or until melted. Add the hot sauce by whisking.

In a big bowl, coat the wings with the butter mixture and serve with the dressing on the side.

CRISPY STICKY TOFU

Prep time:10 minutes

Total time:15minutes

Serving:2

Ingredients

- 300 g extra firm tofu
- 3 tablespoon sweet soy sauce
- 1 tablespoon rice vinegar
- 1-2 garlic cloves
- ½ tablespoon red pepper flakes - or more of you like it spicy
- 4 tablespoon corn starch
- 3-4 tablespoon water
- 3 tablespoon oil
- Garnish sesame seeds or chopped green onions

Instructions

To remove the extra water, drain the tofu and press it either between two clean tea towels or with a tofu press.

Add the sweet soy sauce, vinegar, grated garlic, and chile to a small bowl or ramekin. 3 tablespoons of water and 1 tablespoon of cornstarch should be combined by stirring or whisking.

Place the remaining corn starch on the tofu after cutting it into triangles or cubes.

The tofu pieces should be added in a single layer, making sure they don't touch, and cooking in the oil in a non-stick skillet over medium-high heat. Tofu should be pan-fried until golden and crispy on all sides.

Pour the marinade into the pan; it will start to bubble up immediately. Turn all the tofu pieces over quickly to ensure they are coated on both sides, then serve right away on a platter.

Enjoy your Crispy Sticky Tofu after adding the sesame seeds as a garnish!

AIR FRYER CRAB CAKES

Prep time:15 minutes

Total time:1 hours 15minutes

Serving:2

Ingredients

CRAB CAKES

- 1 large egg
- ¼ c mayonnaise
- 1 tsp mustard powder
- 1 tsp Old Bay seasoning
- ½ tsp white pepper
- ½ tsp salt
- 2 tsp Worcestershire sauce
- 1 lb jumbo lump or lump crab meat, fresh or hand picked
- 10 tbsp panko bread crumbs,
- lemon wedges, for serving

TARTAR SAUCE

- 10 tbsp ½ cup plus 2 tbsp mayonnaise
- ¼ cup minced dill pickle, 3-4 spears
- 1 tbsp fresh dill, patted dry
- 2 tsp lemon juice
- 2 tsp capers

- 1 tbsp Worcestershire sauce
- ¼ tsp mustard powder
- ¼ tsp kosher salt
- ¼ tsp pepper

Instructions

To prepare the tartar sauce. All the components should be mixed thoroughly in a bowl. Once the flavor is perfect, taste it and add salt, pepper, or lemon juice as needed. To help it thicken, chill for at least one hour.

In a sizable mixing bowl, combine the egg, mayonnaise, mustard powder, old bay seasoning, salt, pepper, and Worcestershire sauce.

Cover with the bread crumbs after placing the crab meat on top.

Gently fold the ingredients together with your hands until they almost come together. Refrigerate the mixture for one hour to chill.

Set the air fryer to 400°F for 5 minutes, regardless of whether your equipment requires preheating. Lightly spray with olive oil after preheating.

Scoop half a cup of the chilled crab cake mixture into your palms. Make a crab cake form that is approximately 3" wide and 1" thick. This may need to be done in two sets. Place the crab cakes in an even coating in the air fryer basket, going some span between them. The tops of the crab cakes should be lightly misted with olive oil.

Cook the basket for 5 minutes at 400°F in the air fryer. Cook for another five minutes after turning the crab cakes, or until an instant-read thermometer detects 165°F as the interior temperature.

Take out of the air fryer and serve with tartar sauce and lemon wedges.

AIR FRYER FALAFEL

Prep time:10 minutes

Total time:25minutes

Serving:6

Ingredients

FOR THE TAHINI SAUCE:

- 1/2 cup tahini (I like Joyva)
- 1/4 cup Greek yogurt
- 1/2 lemon, juice only
- 2 tablespoons olive oil
- 1/4 to 1/2 cup hot water

FOR THE FALAFEL:

- 2 (15-ounce) cans chickpeas, rinsed and drained
- 1/4 cup fresh parsley
- 1/4 cup cilantro
- 2 cloves garlic
- 1 large shallot, chopped
- 3 tablespoons all-purpose flour
- 2 tablespoons sesame seeds
- 2 teaspoons ground cumin
- 1 teaspoon paprika
- 1/2 lemon, juice only
- 1 teaspoon salt
- Spray olive oil, for cooking

FOR SERVING:

- 6 pita breads
- Fresh lettuce
- 1 large tomato, sliced thinly

- 1/2 red onion, sliced thinly
- 1 cucumber, sliced thinly

Instructions

MAKE THE TAHINI SAUCE:

Mix the tahini, yogurt, lemon juice, and olive oil in a medium bowl. The mixture will start out being very thick. It should be thinned out with hot water until it is spreadable. To achieve the ideal consistency, slowly add 1/4 to 1/2 cup of boiling water.

MAKE THE FALAFEL MIXTURE:

Add the chickpeas, parsley, cilantro, garlic, shallot, flour, sesame seeds, cumin, paprika, lemon juice, and salt to the food processor's bowl. Pulse the mixture until a loose paste forms. It shouldn't be entirely slick.

Make tablespoon-sized, 1-inch-wide discs out of the falafel mixture. Continue until all of the falafel mixture has been used. Get between 25 and 30 falafel discs.

AIR FRY THE FALAFEL:

Spray some nonstick olive oil on the air fryer basket. Put as many falafel discs as you can into the basket without them touching each other, then lightly mist them with olive oil. For eight minutes, air fried the falafel at 350°F. After flipping, cook the other side for a further six minutes.

Continue until all of the falafel has been cooked.

SERVE THE FALAFEL:

Falafel should be served with warm pita. Serve with your preferred toppings and tahini yogurt sauce!

Falafel leftovers keep well in the refrigerator for 5 to 6 days or can be frozen for longer storage. Falafel should be heated completely in a 350°F oven for 10 to 12 minutes.

AIR FRYER SALMON PATTIES

Prep time:10 minutes

Total time:22 minutes

Serving:4

Ingredients

- 14.75 ounce canned salmon
- 1 large egg
- 3 tablespoons mayonnaise
- ¼ cup panko breadcrumbs
- 1 tablespoon fresh lemon juice
- ½ teaspoon dried dill
- ¼ teaspoon onion powder
- ¼ teaspoon garlic powder
- ¼ teaspoon kosher salt
- ¼ teaspoon ground black pepper
- 1 tablespoon chopped fresh parsley
- Lemon wedges and tartar sauce, for serving

Instructions

Apply cooking spray to the air fryer tray.

Place everything in a large bowl. Mix everything together completely.

Make four patties out of the mixture after dividing it.

Spray some cooking spray on the tops of the salmon patties before placing them in the air fryer tray.

The patties should be thoroughly cooked and golden brown after 10 to 12 minutes of cooking on the air fry setting at 390 degrees F.

Enjoy with tartar sauce and lemon wedges!

AIR-FRYER HAM AND EGG POCKETS

Prep time:25 minutes

Total time:25 minutes

Serving:2

Ingredients

- 1 large egg
- 2 teaspoons 2% milk
- 2 teaspoons butter
- 1 ounce thinly sliced deli ham, chopped
- 2 tablespoons shredded cheddar cheese
- 1 tube refrigerated crescent rolls

Directions

Set air fryer to 300 degrees. Egg and milk should be mixed in a small bowl. Heat the butter in a small skillet until it is hot. Add the egg mixture and whisk continuously over medium heat until the eggs are fully set. Get rid of the heat. Fold in the cheese and ham.

Cut the crescent dough into two rectangles. Seal perforations after spooning half of the filling along the center of each rectangle. Pinch the dough together to secure the fold. Set in an air fryer basket in a single coating on an smooth tray. 8 to 10 minutes, or until light brown.

BONUS SEAFOOD DISHES

SEASONED TILAPIA FILLETS

Prep time:25 minutes

Total time:25 minutes

Serving:2

Ingredients

- 2 tilapia fillets (6 ounces each)
- 1 tablespoon butter, melted
- 1 teaspoon Montreal steak seasoning
- 1/2 teaspoon dried parsley flakes
- 1/4 teaspoon paprika
- 1/4 teaspoon dried thyme
- 1/8 teaspoon onion powder
- 1/8 teaspoon salt
- 1/8 teaspoon pepper
- Dash garlic powder

Directions

the oven to 425 degrees Fahrenheit. Place the tilapia in a prepared 11 x 7-inch baking dish and add butter. Sprinkle remaining components over fillets after mixing in a small gulf.

ten minutes of concealed baking. Restart baking for a further 5 to 8 minutes.

CRISPY FRIED FISH

Prep time:30 minutes

Total time:45 minutes

Serving:4

Ingredients

- 1 egg
- 1 ½ cups beer
- 1 cup all-purpose flour
- 1 teaspoon garlic powder
- ½ teaspoon salt
- ½ teaspoon ground black pepper
- 1 pound cod fillets
- 2 cups crushed cornflake crumbs
- 1 teaspoon Cajun seasoning
- 1 quart oil for frying

Directions

Mix the egg, beer, flour, garlic powder, salt, and pepper in a medium bowl. Cod should be placed in the basin and completely covered with the mixture.

Combine the cornflake crumbs and Cajun seasoning in a different medium bowl. Coat the fish completely on all sides by dipping it in the crumb mixture.

Oil should be heated to 365 degrees F in a sizable, sturdy skillet or deep fryer (185 degrees C). Fry the fish until the flesh can be readily flaked with a fork and is golden brown.

HONEY GARLIC SHRIMP (IN 10 MINUTES!)

Prep time:6 minutes

Total time:10 minutes

Serving:4

Ingredients

- 1 1/2 pounds medium or large shrimp, deveined (tail on or peeled)
- 3 garlic cloves
- ½ teaspoon onion powder
- Heaping ¼ teaspoon kosher salt
- ¼ cup honey
- 3 tablespoons soy sauce
- 1 ½ tablespoons rice vinegar
- 2 teaspoon cornstarch
- 3 tablespoons sesame oil

Instructions

If using frozen shrimp, let them thaw.

Chop up the garlic. To dry, pat the shrimp. Combine it with the kosher salt, onion powder, and minced garlic.

In a little bowl, mix the honey, soy gravy, rice vinegar, and cornstarch. Stir until mostly soft .

Sesame oil should be heated to a medium-high temperature in a big skillet. Turning them with tongs, sauté the shrimp for 1 to 2 minutes until opaque and cooked through.

After removing the shrimp, turn off the heat. While scraping off the browned bits from the pan's bottom, add the glaze to the pan and swirl until it thickens. Stir the shrimp back into the sauce once it has thickened, then serve.

AIR FRYER FISH TACOS WITH CILANTRO LIME SLAW

Prep time:5 minutes

Total time:20 minutes

Serving:4

Ingredients

FOR THE FISH:

- 1 ½ lb tilapia or white fish .
- 1 teaspoon chili powder
- ½ teaspoon oregano
- ½ teaspoon garlic powder
- ½ teaspoon paprika
- ¼ teaspoon cayenne
- ¼ teaspoon onion powder
- ¼ teaspoon cumin
- ½ teaspoon sea salt
- ½ teaspoon cracked pepper

FOR THE CILANTRO LIME SLAW:

- 2½ c cole slaw mix
- 3 T mayonnaise
- 1 T lime juice
- 1 garlic clove, minced
- ⅓ c chopped cilantro
- ½ teaspoon sugar optional
- ¼ sea salt more or less to taste
- ¼ teaspoon cracked pepper

FOR TACO ASSEMBLY:

- tortillas
- extra lime juice

Instructions

Spray oil on the air fryer basket. Mix the spices, salt, and pepper together in a small bowl.

Lay the fish in the air fryer basket after patting it dry. Use olive oil to brush. Spread the spice rub liberally over the fish and gently push it into the flesh. Spray some oil on top of the fish to help everything stick to it and stay moist.

heat the air fryer to 400 degrees. The fish should be heated for around 8 to 10 minutes, or until opaque and flaky. A 145°F internal temperature is ideal.

Combine the ingredients for the cilantro lime salad while the fish cooks. If necessary, add more lime juice or adjust the salt to taste.

Take the cooked fish out of the air fryer basket. Slice into small pieces, add on tortillas, and then sprinkle slaw on top. Increase the amount of lime juice. For two to three days, keep in the refrigerator in an airtight container.

The fish should be heated in the air fryer for 2-4 minutes.

HIBACHI SHRIMP WITH YUM YUM SAUCE

Prep time:15 minutes

Total time:30 minutes

Serving:4

Ingredients

- 1 tablespoon olive oil or other neutral-flavored cooking oil
- 1 pound large or jumbo shrimp, peeled and deveined
- 1 tablespoon soy sauce
- 1 tablespoon lemon juice
- 1/2 cup mayonnaise
- 2 tablespoons ketchup
- 1 teaspoon sugar
- 1/2 teaspoon smoked paprika
- 1/4 teaspoon garlic powder

Instructions

Put the oil in a big skillet or a flat griddle. For a few minutes, heat the oil in the skillet over medium-high heat.

Add the shrimp to the skillet with caution. Turn the shrimp over after 2 minutes of cooking. Let the shrimp cook for a further two minutes in the skillet before adding the soy sauce and lemon juice.

To transfer the shrimp to a serving plate, use tongs.

Mayonnaise, ketchup, sugar, paprika, and garlic powder should be mixed together in a small bowl to form the sauce. To blend, stir.

With the Yum Yum Sauce on the side, serve the cooked shrimp with your choice of cooked vegetables, rice, or noodles.

BAKED HONEY SRIRACHA LIME SALMON

Prep time:15 minutes

Total time:30 minutes

Serving:4

Ingredients

- 1 large salmon - or 4-6 separate fillets
- salt and pepper to taste –
- 2 tablespoons butter
- ⅓ cup honey
- ⅓ cup sriracha
- 2 limes
- 2 tablespoons soy sauce
- 1 teaspoon minced garlic
- 1 tablespoon freshly chopped cilantro

Instructions

A 400 degree oven is recommended. Salmon should be placed on a baking sheet lined with foil, gently greased. Add salt and pepper to taste while preparing fish. Slice a lime thinly, then tuck the slices under the salmon's edges.

Melt butter in a medium sauce pan over medium-high heat. Add honey, sriracha sauce, lime juice, soy sauce, and garlic to the mixture. Get to a boil, lower warmth to medium, and simmer for an additional 3 to 4 minutes.

Use a ladle or spatula to spread the remaining sauce evenly over the salmon after running over 2/3 of it.

To prevent the sauce from dripping all over the place, fold the foil's edges up around the salmon.

After 15 minutes of baking, turn to broiling and cook the salmon for a further 4–5 minutes, or until the very edges start to lightly sear. Be cautious not to let the salmon burn on the bottom.

Serve fish topped with the saved sauce and chopped cilantro.

BONUS VEGETABLE DISHES

LENTIL FALAFEL BURGER RECIPE WITH CREAMY FETA SAUCE

Prep time: 45 minutes

Total time:55 minutes

Serving:4

Ingredients

FOR THE BURGERS:

- ⅓ cup dry black beluga lentils
- 1 cup cooked chickpeas
- ½ medium sweet potato
- peeled and cut into ½-inch cubes
- 4 cups water
- ½ small red onion
- finely chopped
- 1 large egg
- ⅔ cup whole-wheat panko breadcrumbs
- ¼ cup fresh cilantro
- 4 teaspoons sesame seeds
- 1 tablespoon ground cumin
- 1 teaspoon ground coriander
- 3 cloves garlic, peeled and minced
- 2 teaspoons dried marjoram
- 1 teaspoon dried oregano
- ½ teaspoon ground sumac
- optional
- 1½ teaspoons salt

- ½ teaspoon ground black pepper
- Nonstick pan spray

FOR THE TOPPINGS/BURGER BUNS:

- 4 whole wheat or sprouted wheat burger buns
- 2-3 vine-ripened tomatoes
- cored and thinly sliced
- Sliced cucumber
- Diced red onions
- Fresh baby spinach

FOR THE FETA-MINT-YOGURT SAUCE:

- 3 tablespoons crumbled feta cheese
- ½ cup plain low-fat yogurt
- 2 tablespoons finely chopped fresh mint leaves

Instructions

MAKE THE BURGERS:

Lentils, sweet potatoes, and water should be combined in a medium saucepan and heated to a rolling boil. After about 25 minutes, lower the heat to medium-low and gently boil the potatoes and lentils until they are cooked. Drain the combination.

The lentil mixture should be added to a food processor. Add the onion, egg, panko breadcrumbs, salt, and pepper to the lentil mixture. Five 1-second pulses should be plenty to roughly chop the food.

Form the ingredients into four patties that are between 4 and 412 inches long and 12 inch thick.

A sizable nonstick skillet should be heated to medium. Apply two of the lentil patties to the skillet after lightly misting it with nonstick cooking spray. 3 to 4 minutes of browning the burgers, then flip and cook for another 3 minutes on the other side. Repeat the process with the remaining patties, then transfer to a large plate.

MAKE THE SAUCE:

The feta cheese should be added to a medium bowl and crumbled using a fork. Add the yogurt and mint, and stir.

A lentil burger, some feta sauce, and your vegetables should be placed on each of the four bottoms of the burgers. Add the remaining hamburger buns on top. Serve right away

ZUCCHINI BURGERS

Prep time: 15 minutes

Total time:30 minutes

Serving:4

Ingredients

- 2 cups shredded zucchini
- 1 medium onion, finely chopped
- 1/2 cup dry bread crumbs
- 2 large eggs, lightly beaten
- 1/8 teaspoon salt
- Dash cayenne pepper
- 3 hard-boiled large egg whites, chopped
- 2 tablespoons canola oil
- 4 whole wheat hamburger buns, split
- 4 lettuce leaves
- 4 slices tomato
- 4 slices onion
-

Directions

Squeeze zucchini to drain extra liquid in a strainer or colander. Clean off. Combine the zucchini, onion, bread crumbs, eggs, salt, and cayenne in a small bowl. Add chopped egg whites slowly while stirring.

In a large nonstick skillet over medium-low warmth, warm 1 tablespoon of oil. By light 2/3 cupfuls, dip batter into oil; gently press to flatten. Using the remaining oil as needed, fry the food in batches until golden brown on both sides.

Serve with lettuce, tomato, and onion on buns.

ITALIAN TURKEY ZUCCHINI MEATBALLS

Prep time: 10 minutes

Total time:25 minutes

Serving:28

Ingredients

- 2 lb. 93/7 lean ground turkey
- 2 cups shredded zucchini, loosely packed
- 2 tsp. dried Italian Seasoning
- 2 tsp. garlic powder
- 1 tsp. onion powder
- 1/2 tsp. crushed red pepper flakes
- 1 tsp. sea salt
- 1/2 tsp. black pepper

Instructions

400°F for the oven's temperature. Use parchment paper to line a sizable baking sheet. Place aside.

To absorb moisture from the shredded zucchini, spread the zucchini out on one half of a double sheet of paper towels, cover it with another double layer, or fold the paper towel over the zucchini and push down with your hands.

In a bowl, combine all the ingredients and stir with a spoon or your hands.

Place on the baking sheet in the shape of 28 meatballs that are around the size of a golf ball and 1 1/2 ounces each.

Bake the meatballs for 18 to 20 minutes, or until they are done and the insides are no longer pink.

Serve without any additional sauce or with your preferred marinara. Primal Kitchen Marinara Sauce is great!

QUICK MACARONI QUICHE

Prep time: 15 minutes

Total time:1 hour 10 minutes

Serving: 5

Ingredients

- 1 packet puff pastry from the refrigerated shelf (275 g)
- 180 g peas, frozen
- 100 g cooked ham
- 200 g macaroni
- 200 g Gouda cheese, rated
- 5 egg
- 400 g sour cream
- 100 ml Cremefine or other low-fat cream
- 3 teaspoons parsley, frozen
- salt and pepper
- nutmeg
- 6 cherry tomato
- some fat for the shape
- some flour for the work surface

Instructions

Cook the pasta as required on the packet in salted water, then empty completely. Set the oven's fan temperature to 180 ° C. Slice the ham.

In a bowl, combine the macaroni, ham, peas, and 100 g of Gouda cheese.

Roll out the puff pastry rectangle until it is approximately 35 x 35 cm long, sprinkle some flour on the work area, and then fold it up.

Put the puff pastry in a springform pan that has been greased, and create a 5 cm high edge around it. Use a fork to make holes in the bottom. In the springform pan, layer the batter with the macaroni, ham, peas, and cheese.

In a bowl, combine the 5 eggs with the sour cream, cream, pepper, salt, and nutmeg. Pour this mixture over the mixture in the springform pan. Cherry tomatoes should be cut in half and added to the quiche.

Bake the quiche for 45 minutes on the bottom rack, then sprinkle the remaining 100 g of Gouda cheese on top. After baking, top with parsley and allow to stand for approximately 10 minutes.

It also tastes wonderful to make a quick tomato sauce using strained tomatoes, pepper, vegetable stock, Italian herbs, and a dash of sugar.

BONUS BEEF RECIPES

STUFFED MEATLOAF

Prep time: 35 minutes

Total time:2 hour 20 minutes

Serving: 8

Ingredients

- 1½ lbs ground beef
- ¾ cup quick oatmeal
- ¾ cup milk
- 1 egg
- ½ cup finely chopped onion
- 1¼ tsp salt
- ¼ tsp pepper
- 1 package chicken Stove-Top stuffing prepared according to package instructions

FOR THE MUSHROOM GRAVY

- 1 8 ounce pkg of fresh mushrooms, sliced thinly
- ¼ cup finely diced onion
- 1 tbsp olive oil or butter
- 2 (10.5 ounce) cans of Balm of Mushroom Soup
- 1½ cups milk
- salt and pepper

Instructions

In a sizable mixing basin, combine the ground beef, oats, milk, onion, egg, salt, and pepper to make the meatloaf. Mix and combine everything into the meat with your hands. Avoid overmixing. It will take between 30 and 60 seconds.

Place plastic wrap over a flat area of your countertop. I create a sheet of plastic that is around 18 inches by 24 inches by overlapping two strips. View the step-by-step photo collage for images.

The combined meatloaf should be placed in the center of the plastic wrap and should be pressed down to form a broad rectangle. The meat combination should be between 12 and 34 of an inch thick.

You now spread the prepared stuffing equally over the entire rectangle of meatloaf after forming a good rectangle (about 12x18 inches, give or take a little).

To help the stuffing stick to the meatloaf at this time, gently press it down. You are now prepared to roll it up.

Roll the rectangle over on itself by raising the edge with the aid of the plastic wrap. Put the meatloaf in there as firmly as you can without tearing or breaking it. Check at the images to see how this is done.

Once it is nicely rolled, use your hands to gently clamp down the corners.

You now need to get the pan you're going to fry it on ready. You can see from the photos that I lined a cookie sheet with foil before placing slices of bread down the middle to rest the meatloaf on. Because I don't have a broiler pan with me in Germany, I did this. A portion of the top of a broiler pan drains. Normally, I'd spray that with cooking spray, put my meatloaf on top of it, and let all the extra grease drip to the bottom of the pan. I don't have one, so I put the bread slices on top of the meatloaf so they can soak up the additional grease. Works perfectly.

It can be a little challenging to get the meatloaf onto the oven sheet. I delicately roll it onto the pan where I want it, in my case on top of the bread pieces, using the plastic wrap to pick it up.

I would now advise chilling the meatloaf (covered tightly with plastic wrap for 3-4 hours.) By doing this, the flesh is solidified and is less likely to crack while cooking. It's fine if you decide not to refrigerate it, but there is a good chance that it will crack while cooking. When I don't care about how it appears or how the taste is affected, I never put food in the refrigerator. I did, however, chill it for these photos.

When the time is right, preheat the oven to 350 degrees and bake the meatloaf uncovered for 1 hour and 45 minutes.

Before slicing, let the meatloaf rest for 15 to 20 minutes.

INSTRUCTIONS FOR MUSHROOM GRAVY:

Sliced mushrooms and diced onion should be sauteed in butter or olive oil in a medium saute pan. While sautéing, season with salt and pepper.

Add the milk and cream of mushroom soup once the mushrooms are soft. Well combine, then bring to a boil. Simmer for 3 to 5 minutes after reducing to a simmer. Depending on the required consistency, add more milk. If necessary, season with salt and pepper as well.

With mashed potatoes or a baked potato and gravy on top, serve meatloaf. SO DELISH!

CHEESE-STUFFED BURGERS FOR TWO

Prep time: 25 minutes

Total time:25 minutes

Serving: 2

Ingredients

- 1 tablespoon finely chopped onion
- 1 tablespoon ketchup
- 1 teaspoon prepared mustard
- 1/4 teaspoon salt
- 1/8 teaspoon pepper
- 1/2 pound lean ground beef
- 1/4 cup finely shredded cheddar cheese
- 2 hamburger buns, split
- Optional: Lettuce leaves and tomato slices

Directions

Combine the first five ingredients in a small bowl. Over the mixture, crumble the beef, and stir gently but completely. 4 thin patties should be formed. Two patties should have cheese on them. Add the remaining patties on top, sealing the edges tightly.

Cover the burgers and grill them for 5–6 minutes per side. If desired, serve on buns with lettuce and tomato on top.

BEEF SCHNITZEL

Prep time: 20 minutes

Total time:40 minutes

Serving: 5

Ingredients

- 5 thin-cut minute steaks
- 50g plain flour
- 2 tsp paprika
- 2 eggs, lightly beaten
- 250g dried breadcrumbs
- 5 tsp butter
- 5 tsp olive oil
- lemon wedges, to serve

Directions

The steaks should be placed on top of a piece of cling film that has been stretched over a cutting board, followed by another piece of cling film. The steaks should be pounded with a rolling pin until they are extremely flat and thin.

On a plate, combine the flour, paprika, salt, and pepper. Dip the steaks in the flour first, then the egg, and finally the breadcrumbs on two more plates.

One of the schnitzels should be cooked for about a minute on each side until the breadcrumbs are golden and crispy. Warmth 1 tablespoon of butter and 1 tablespoon of oil in a broad frying pan. For the additional schnitzels, repeat Step 3. If desired, serve with salad, coleslaw, and lemon wedges.

GRILLED ASPARAGUS STEAK BUNDLES

Prep time: 20 minutes

Total time: 30 minutes

Serving: 2

Ingredients

- ½ pound thin skirt steak, cut of extra fat
- 1 tablespoon Montreal steak condiment
- ½ pound thin asparagus pikes, trimmed
- 1 teaspoon olive oil
- salt and ground black pepper to flavour
- ⅓ cup grated Parmesan cheese
- ½ jarred roasted red pepper, cut into six 1/2-inch ribbons
- 6 toothpicks
- 1 tablespoon ground Parmesan cheese

Directions

Use a meat mallet to butterfly or pound steak to a thickness of 1/4 inch. 6 strips, each measuring about 2 inches broad by 5 inches long, should be cut. Place in the fridge after seasoning both sides with Montreal steak seasoning.

On the "Grill" setting, preheat the Panasonic Countertop Induction Oven to medium-high.

Put the asparagus in a shallow dish and cover with the oil. Add salt and pepper to taste.

Asparagus should be grilled for two minutes, flipping after one. Place on a platter.

On the "Grill" setting, rewarm the induction oven to medium-high.

Steak strips should be arranged in a line close to one another. Add 1/3 cup of Parmesan cheese evenly. On top, arrange 3 to 4 spears of asparagus perpendicular to each steak strip. Add one red pepper strip to the asparagus.

To prevent the steak from touching the asparagus, roll it tightly around it. Use a toothpick to secure.

Turning the steak bundles every two minutes, grill for 8 minutes. Put on a platter and top with a spoonful of Parmesan cheese.

JUICIEST HAMBURGERS EVER

Prep time: 15 minutes

Total time: 35 minutes

Serving: 8

Ingredients

- 2 pounds ground beef
- 1 egg, beaten
- ¾ cup dry bread crumbs
- 3 tablespoons evaporated milk
- 2 tablespoons Worcestershire sauce
- ⅛ teaspoon cayenne pepper
- 2 cloves garlic, minced

Directions

Heat a grill to a high temperature.

Use your hands to thoroughly combine the ground beef, egg, bread crumbs, evaporated milk, Worcestershire sauce, cayenne pepper, and garlic in a big bowl. The combination should yield 8 hamburger patties.

Give the grill grate a little oil. About 5 minutes per side, grill patties until browned and no longer pink.

VEGETABLE STEAK KABOBS

Prep time: 20 minutes

Total time: 30 minutes

Serving: 6

Ingredients

- 1/2 cup olive oil
- 1/3 cup red wine vinegar
- 2 tablespoons ketchup
- 2 to 3 garlic cloves, minced
- 1 teaspoon Worcestershire sauce
- 1/2 teaspoon each dried marjoram, basil and oregano
- 1/2 teaspoon dried rosemary, crushed
- 1 beef top sirloin steak (1-1/2 pounds), cut into 1-inch cubes
- 1/2 pound whole fresh mushrooms
- 2 medium onions, cut into wedges
- 1-1/2 cups cherry tomatoes
- 2 small green peppers, cut into 1-inch pieces

Directions

In a small bowl, combine the seasonings, Worcestershire sauce, ketchup, vinegar, oil, and vinegar. Place 1/2 cup of the marinade in a large, sealable plastic bag. Close the bag and shake to coat the beef. Place any remaining marinade in a second large, sealable plastic bag. Add the peppers, tomatoes, mushrooms, and onions to the bag and seal it. Beef and vegetables must be refrigerated for at least eight hours.

Drain beef and throw away marinade. Vegetables should be drained; save marinade for basting. Thread steak and veggies alternately onto six skewers made of metal or moistened wood.

When the meat is the proper doneness and the vegetables are crisp-tender, grill the kabobs, covered, over medium heat or broil them 4 inches from the heat for 10-15 minutes, turning them occasionally. During the final five minutes, baste with the reserved marinade.

PAN-FRIED RIB-EYE STEAK

Prep time: 5 minutes

Total time: 15 minutes

Serving: 2

Ingredients

- 2 rib-eye steaks, each about 200g and 2cm thick
- 1tbsp sunflower oil
- 1 tbsp/25g butter
- 1 garlic clove, left unharmed but bashed once
- thyme, optional

Directions

Use document towels to pat the steaks dehydrated and season with salt and pepper up to eight hours before boiling. In a heavy-bottomed frying pan big enough to hold both steaks comfortably, heat the oil over a high burner. Reduce the heat to medium-high and add the butter when the oil begins to shimmer. Lay the steaks carefully in the pan once it begins to sizzle, tucking the garlic and herbs in at the sides.

With a pair of tongs, stand over the steaks and sear and turn them every 30 to 1 minute or so to give them a good brown crust. As a general rule, each steak will require a total of 4 minutes for rare, 5-6 minutes for medium, and 8-10 minutes for well-done. If you have a digital cookery thermometer, the seat of the steak should be at 50 phases Celsius for rare, 60 phases Celsius for medium, and 70 phases Celsius for well-done. Give the steaks at least five minutes to rest. You can prepare a traditional red wine sauce to go with the steaks while they are resting.

HEALTHY SLOPPY JOES

Prep time: 5 minutes

Total time: 25 minutes

Serving: 4

Ingredients

- 1 yellow onion
- 1 celery rib or green onion
- 1 tablespoon olive oil
- 1 15-ounce can kidney beans
- 1 15-ounce can pinto beans
- 1 15-ounce can tomato sauce
- ½ cup organic ketchup
- 2 tablespoons vegan Worcestershire sauce
- 1 tablespoon apple cider vinegar
- 2 teaspoons chili powder
- 1 teaspoon garlic powder
- 1 teaspoon oregano
- ½ teaspoon kosher salt
- Fresh ground pepper
- Dash hot sauce

Instructions

Chop the celery and onion finely. Olive oil should be heated in a skillet. Add the onion and celery, and sauté for 4 to 5 minutes, or until tender.

Let the beans drain. In the same skillet, combine the kidney beans, pinto beans, tomato sauce, ketchup, Worcestershire sauce, apple cider vinegar, chili powder, garlic powder, oregano, kosher salt, and black pepper. Simmer for 5 to 10 minutes, or until the mixture thickens. If necessary, taste and adjust the seasoning.

Serve with vinegar coleslaw or creamy coleslaw, as desired, on a toasted bun.

BEEF CURRY

Prep time: 20 minutes

Total time: 2 hours 30 minutes

Serving: 4

Ingredients

- 2 tbsp oil
- 500g diced braising steak
- 1 tbsp butter
- 1 large onion, chopped
- 2 garlic cloves, crushed
- 1 thumb sized piece of ginger, finely grated
- ¼ tsp hot chilli powder
- 1 tsp turmeric
- 2 tsp ground coriander
- 3 cardamom pods, crushed
- 400g can chopped tomatoes
- 300ml beef stock
- 1 tsp sugar
- 2 tsp garam masala
- 2 tbsp double cream
- ½ small bunch coriander, roughly chopped
- naan bread or rice, to serve

Instructions

In a casserole pot, heat one tablespoon of the oil to medium-high. When the meat is evenly browned, season it and cook it in the pot for 5-8 minutes, rotating it with a pair of tongs halfway through. On a dish, set aside.

The onions are then added to the pan along with the remaining butter and oil. 15 minutes of gentle frying will produce golden brown and caramelized food. Fry for two minutes after adding the garlic, ginger, chilli, turmeric, ground coriander, and cardamom. Add the tomatoes, stock, and sugar, then boil the mixture.

Add the beef, cover the pan with a lid, and simmer the curry for 1 1/2 to 2 hours. For the final 20 minutes of cooking, remove the lid.

Add the cream and garam masala, then season to taste. Add the coriander and serve with rice or naan flatbread.

GRILLED STEAK SALAD WITH SESAME DRESSING

Prep time: 30 minutes

Total time: 1 hours 45 minutes

Serving: 2

Ingredients

- 1 rib eye steak
- 1 tablespoon soy sauce
- 1 teaspoon Montreal steak seasoning,
- ½ lemon, juiced
- 2 tablespoons rice vinegar
- 2 tablespoons olive oil
- 2 tablespoons white sugar
- ½ teaspoon sesame oil
- ¼ teaspoon garlic powder
- 2 pinches red pepper flakes
- 10 leaves romaine lettuce, torn into bite-size pieces

- ½ large English cucumber, cubed
- 1 avocado - peeled, pitted, and diced
- 1 tomato, cut into wedges
- 1 carrot, grated
- 4 thin slices red onion
- 3 tablespoons toasted sesame seeds

Directions

The rib-eye steak is seasoned on both sides with soy gravy and steak spice. Cover it up and put it in the fridge for at slightly an hour and up to 24 hours.

Set an outdoor grill over medium-high heat and give the grates a quick oiling.

Grill steak for six minutes on each side, or until it is firm, reddish-pink, and juicy throughout. The inside temperature should register 130 degrees Fahrenheit on an instant-read thermometer (54 degrees C). Put the steak on a serving tray, top with lemon juice, and cover loosely with foil. After letting the meat rest for approximately 10 minutes, cut it into strips.

In a small bowl, combine the rice vinegar, olive oil, sugar, sesame oil, garlic powder, and red pepper flakes. In a large bowl, mix the steak strips, lettuce, cucumber, avocado, tomato, carrot, and red onion. Toss the salad in the rice vinegar dressing before serving. To serve, top with sesame seeds.

SUNDAY POT ROAST WITH MUSHROOM GRAVY

Prep time: 5 minutes

Total time: 3 hours 5 minutes

Serving: 4

Ingredients

- 1 (4 to 5-pound) boneless beef bottom round roast
- Kosher salt and freshly ground black pepper
- 2 tablespoons olive oil
- 1 pound cremini mushrooms, cleaned and quartered
- 2 medium yellow onions, halved and sliced
- 4 cups low-sodium beef broth

Directions

Set the oven's temperature to 325 F.

Use paper towels to pat the meat dry before liberally seasoning it with salt and pepper on all sides. Over medium-high heat, add the oil to a sizable Dutch oven, add the roast, and cook for 4 minutes on each side to brown all sides. Place the mushrooms on a platter with the meat. Add salt and pepper, then simmer for approximately 5 minutes, stirring periodically, until browned and starting to release liquid.

Stir in the broth after adding the onions. Insert the roast into the vegetables, releasing any juices into the cooking vessel. To roast for 2 1/2 hours, add the beef stock, bring to a simmer, cover, and place in the oven. After 30 minutes of cooking, take off the top, carefully flip the meat, and check to see whether the liquid has diminished and the flesh is fork-tender.

The meat should be moved to a chopping board and covered with foil to keep it warm once the pot has been taken out of the oven. Allow the mushrooms and onions to stand unattended for a few minutes so that some of the beef fat can float to the top. Skim the extra fat off with a big spoon and throw it away. About 1 1/2 cups of the mushrooms and onions, along with some cooking liquid, should be added to the bowl of a blender or food processor with a ladle. Blend the mixture slowly and thoroughly. Once mixed, pour the puree back into the pot and stir vigorously. Taste and correct the seasoning.

Slice the pot roast and place it on a serving plate to serve. Pass the extra gravy around the table and drizzle some mushroom gravy on top.

GRILLED STEAK FAJITA BOWLS

Prep time: 15 minutes

Total time: 2 hours 35 minutes

Serving: 4

Ingredients

FOR THE MARINADE

- Zest of 2 oranges
- Juice of 3 oranges, 1 cup
- Zest of 2 limes
- Juice of 2 limes, 2 tablespoons
- 1/3 cup (78 ml) red or white wine vinegar
- 1/3 cup (78ml) fresh cilantro
- 1 green onions, chopped
- 2 tablespoons soy sauce
- 1 teaspoon garlic powder or 1 garlic clove
- 2 teaspoons ground cumin
- 1 teaspoon smoked paprika
- 1 teaspoon Mexican oregano
- 2 teaspoons chili powder
- 1 teaspoon salt
- 1/2 teaspoon ground black pepper
- 2 pounds (1 kg) flank or skirt steak

FOR THE VEGETABLES

- 1 teaspoon chili powder
- 1/2 teaspoon ground cumin
- 1 teaspoon salt
- 1/2 teaspoon ground black pepper
- 3 tablespoons vegetable oil

- 2 red peppers, sliced
- 2 yellow peppers, sliced
- 2 yellow onions, sliced
- Quick and Easy Grilled Corn Salsa
- Black beans
- 2 avocados, sliced
- Your favorite salsa

Instructions

FOR THE MARINADE:

Orange and lime juice, orange and lime zest, vinegar, cilantro, green onion, soy sauce, garlic, cumin, smoked paprika, oregano, chili powder, salt, and pepper should all be added to a blender or food processor. Until smooth, blend.

Count the steak and marinade to a big zip-top bag. For at least two hours up to overnight, cover and chill.

Heat the grill.

While the grill is heating, remove the steak from the marinade and let it rest at room temperature.

FOR THE PEPPERS AND ONIONS:

Add the chili powder, cumin, salt, and pepper to a small bowl. Blend in the oil.

In a bowl, combine the oil and spices with the peppers and onions.

Add the steak to the grill once it is heated. For medium, grill for 5 to 6 minutes on the first side and 4 minutes on the other. Transfer off the grill to a cutting board, then let cool.

The peppers and onions should be added to the grill and tossed until they are cooked and slightly browned. Remove.

Crossing the grain, thinly slice the steak. Serve the peppers, onions, corn salsa, black beans, avocado, and your preferred salsa on a bed of chopped lettuce or rice.

AIR-FRYER CHICKEN PARMESAN

Prep time: 15 minutes

Total time: 2 hours 35 minutes

Serving: 4

Ingredients

- 2 large eggs
- 1/2 cup seasoned bread crumbs
- 1/3 cup grated Parmesan cheese
- 1/4 teaspoon pepper
- 4 boneless skinless chicken breast halves
- 1 cup pasta sauce
- 1 cup shredded mozzarella cheese
- Optional: Chopped fresh basil and hot cooked pasta

Directions

the air fryer to 375 degrees. Eggs should be lightly beaten in a small basin. Combine bread crumbs, Parmesan cheese, and pepper in another small bowl. Chicken is dipped in egg, then is coated with the crumb mixture.

Set the chicken in the air fryer basket in a single coating on an smooth tray. Cook for 10–12 minutes, rotating once, or until an instant-read thermometer registers 165°. Add sauce and cheese to the chicken. Cook for 3–4 more minutes, or until cheese is melted. Add more Parmesan cheese and chopped basil, if preferred, and serve with spaghetti.

AIR FRYER COD RECIPE

Prep time: 2 minutes

Total time: 15 minutes

Serving: 4

Ingredients

- 1 Lb Cod Fillets
- 1 Tablespoon Oil
- Salt/Pepper - to taste
- 2 Lemons - sliced thin
- 2 teaspoons Fresh Chopped Dill

Instructions

Apply salt, pepper, and oil to the cod fillets.

air fryer basket with spray.

Add lemon slices to the basket. On top of the lemon slices, arrange the fish fillets.

Each fillet should have a slice of lemon on top.

Cook fish in an air fryer at 400°F for 10–13 minutes. The consistency of the fish fillets and the air fryer being used will affect how long the meals will take to cook.

Add chopped dill on top before serving cod.

AIR FRYER STEAK

Prep time: 10 minutes

Total time: 30 minutes

Serving: 2

Ingredients

- 1-2 Ribeye New York,
- 1 tablespoon olive oil
- 1 teaspoon Italian seasoning
- salt and pepper

GARLIC HERB BUTTER:

- 1/4 cup butter softened
- 1 garlic clove minced
- 1 teaspoon fresh rosemary
- 1 teaspoon fresh thyme
- 1 teaspoon fresh parsley

Instructions

400 degrees should be the air fryer's setting. Rub some olive oil on both sides of the steaks to prepare them. On both sides, rub salt, pepper, and Italian seasoning.

When the steak is medium, add it to the air fryer basket and cook for 12 minutes before turning it over. Ten minutes after the steak has rested, top with garlic butter.

AIR FRYER ROAST PORK

Prep time: 10 minutes

Total time: 1 hours 20 minutes

Serving: 6

Ingredients

- 1.5kg Roast Pork Leg or Shoulder
- 1 tablespoon Olive Oil
- 1-2 tablespoon Coarse Salt

Instructions

Your roast should be taken out of the packing and any netting before being dried with paper towels. Score the rind with a tiny, sharp knife at 1-cm intervals, being careful not to cut into the meat. Get your butcher to score your rind for you as an alternative.

If time permits, store the meat in the refrigerator unwrapped for the night. Rub olive oil all over the pork before roasting. Next, liberally sprinkle the rind with salt, being sure to press it into the ridges.

Put the roast in the air fryer basket with the rind up and cook for 20 minutes at 200°C (400°F), then for another 20 minutes at 180°C (350°F) until thoroughly done. Place the roast on a cutting board or platter and give it 10 minutes to rest. Carve, then dish.

AIR FRYER NAAN PIZZA

Prep time: 2 minutes

Total time: 9 minutes

Serving: 4

Ingredients

- 4 pieces mini naan - or one regular-sized naan, if your air fryer can accommodate it
- ¼ cup pizza sauce of your choice - I used garlic-infused olive oil
- 6 oz mozzarella cheese - or shredded cheese blend of your choice
- toppings of your choice - veggies, pepperoni, sausage, etc.

Instructions

Naan should be placed in a single layer in the air fryer's basket or on the rack. Work in groups if required.

Four small naan breads

2 minutes at 370°F or until the edges are just beginning to turn somewhat crispy. Carefully remove from air fryer.

Pizza sauce, cheese, and any additional toppings of your choosing should be spread onto the naan pieces. Back at the air fryer.

For a further five minutes, air fried at 370°F, or until the cheese is melted and the naan are browned and crispy.

AIR FRYER BREAKFAST SANDWICHES

Prep time: 10 minutes

Total time:10 minutes

Serving: 1

Ingredients

- 1 Frozen Breakfast Sandwich

Instructions

The breakfast sandwich should be divided in half. Ride the fill over so that the cheese is following to the bread.

Place the two halves, bread side down and meat and egg side up, in the air fryer basket. 340°F/170°C air fry for 6 to 8 minutes.

Put the breakfast sandwich back together. The bread should now be brown after another 2 minutes of air frying at 340°F.

AIR FRYER LEMON PEPPER SHRIMP

Prep time: 5 minutes

Total time:15 minutes

Serving: 2

Ingredients

- 1 tablespoon olive oil
- 1 lemon, juiced
- 1 teaspoon lemon pepper
- ¼ teaspoon paprika
- ¼ teaspoon garlic powder
- 12 ounces uncooked medium shrimp, peeled and deveined
- 1 lemon, sliced

Directions

As directed by the manufacturer, heat an air fryer to 400 degrees F .

In a bowl, mix the oil, paprika, garlic powder, lemon juice, and lemon pepper. Add the shrimp and coat well.

Cook shrimp in the preheated air fryer for 6 to 8 minutes, or until the meat is opaque and the shrimp are brilliant pink on the outside. Add lemon wedges to the dish.

CRISPY AIR FRYER "FRIED" CHICKEN

Prep time: 10 minutes

Total time:40 minutes

Serving: 4

Ingredients

- 1-2 pounds bone-in chicken thighs and legs
- salt and pepper
- 2 cups buttermilk
- 2 eggs
- 2 cups flour
- 1 Tablespoon cajun seasoning
- 1 Tablespoon garlic powder
- 1 teaspoon onion powder
- 2 teaspoons paprika
- 1 teaspoon salt
- 1 teaspoon pepper
- olive oil spray

Instructions

Chicken thighs and legs with salt and pepper. Add the eggs and buttermilk to a medium bowl and whisk to mix. Count the flour, cajun, garlic powder, onion powder, paprika, salt, and pepper to another medium-sized bowl.

Dredge the chicken in the flour, then the buttermilk, and finally the flour using tongs. Put in the air fryer basket's bottom.

Cook for 15 to 20 minutes at 360 degrees. To remove any flour, open the basket and spray it with cooking spray. When the chicken is 165 degrees and no longer pink, turn it over and cook for an additional 5 to 10 minutes.

AIR-FRYER SOUTHERN-STYLE CHICKEN

Prep time: 15 minutes

Total time:35 minutes

Serving: 6

Ingredients

- 2 cups crushed Ritz crackers
- 1 tablespoon minced fresh parsley
- 1 teaspoon garlic salt
- 1 teaspoon paprika
- 1/2 teaspoon pepper
- 1/4 teaspoon ground cumin
- 1/4 teaspoon rubbed sage
- 1 large egg, beaten
- 1 broiler/fryer chicken , cut up
- Cooking spray

Directions

the air fryer to 375 degrees. Mix the first 7 ingredients in a small dish. Put the egg in a different, small bowl. After dipping the chicken in the egg, coat it with the cracker mixture by patting it down. Chicken should be placed in single layers on a oiled tray in the air fryer basket and spread with cooking mist in batches.

10 minutes to cook. Rush cookery spray after turning the chicken. Cook for 10–20 minutes more, or until the chicken is golden brown and the liquids are clear.

SWEET AND SPICY AIR-FRYER MEATBALLS

Prep time: 30 minutes

Total time:45 minutes

Serving: 3 dozon

Ingredients

- 2/3 cup quick-cooking oats
- 1/2 cup crushed Ritz crackers
- 2 large eggs, lightly beaten
- 1 can evaporated milk
- 1 tablespoon dried minced onion
- 1 teaspoon salt
- 1 teaspoon garlic powder
- 1 teaspoon ground cumin
- 1 teaspoon honey
- 1/2 teaspoon pepper
- 2 pounds lean ground beef

SAUCE:

- 1/3 cup packed brown sugar
- 1/3 cup honey
- 1/3 cup orange marmalade
- 2 tablespoons cornstarch
- 2 tablespoons soy sauce
- 1 to 2 tablespoons Louisiana-style hot sauce
- 1 tablespoon Worcestershire sauce

Directions

the air fryer to 380 degrees. Combine the first 10 ingredients in a big bowl. Add the steak and stir just enough to combine. Form into 1-1/2" balls.

Meatballs should be arranged in a single layer in the air fryer basket on a greased tray in batches. Cook for 12 to 15 minutes. In the meantime, combine the sauce's components in a small pan. Over medium heat, whisk and cook until thickened. accompany with meatballs.

WHITE SAUCE

Prep time: 2 minutes

Total time:17 minutes

Serving: 1 cup

Ingredients

- 500ml whole milk
- 1 onion, halved
- 1 bay leaf
- 2 cloves
- 50g butter
- 50g plain flour

Directions

With the onion, bay leaf, and cloves added, get the milk to a spot in a little saucepan. After 20 minutes, turn off the heat and let the mixture steep.

In a another pot, melt the butter before melding in the all-purpose flour. The term "roux" refers to the paste that formed after prolonged stirring. Cook for another two minutes.

With a slotted spoon, remove the onion, bay, and cloves from the milk and throw them away. As you gently whisk in the infused milk to the roux, you can achieve a silky sauce. Cook with constant stirring for 5 to 10 minutes, or until the sauce has thickened. according to taste.

SIDES DESHES

AIR-FRYER GARLIC BREAD

Prep time: 5 minutes

Total time:20 minutes

Serving: 8

Ingredients

- 1/4 cup butter, softened
- 3 tablespoons grated Parmesan cheese
- 2 garlic cloves, minced
- 2 teaspoons minced fresh parsley or 1/2 teaspoon dried parsley flakes
- 8 slices ciabatta or French bread

Directions

the air fryer to 350 degrees. Spread over bread after combining the first 4 ingredients in a small bowl.

Place the bread on the tray in the air fryer basket in batches. Cook for 2 to 3 minutes or until golden brown. Serve hot.

15 MINUTE CRISPY AIR FRYER CHICKPEAS

Prep time: 5 minutes

Total time:15 minutes

Serving: 3

Ingredients

- 1 14-oz can chickpeas 425g
- 1 Tbsp olive oil 15 mL
- ½ tsp salt or seasoning of choice,

Instructions

Prepare chickpeas by draining and drying them with paper towels. Salt and oil are combined and stirred.

Cook: Arrange in a single layer in the basket or rack of your air fryer. Cook for 8 to 10 minutes.

AIR FRYER ROASTED POTATOES

Prep time: 5 minutes

Total time:25 minutes

Serving: 4

Ingredients

- 1 pound Yukon gold baby potatoes cut into one inch pieces
- 2 Tablespoons olive oil
- 1/2 Tablespoon Italian Seasoning
- 3 cloves garlic minced
- salt and pepper
- 1/4 cup shredded parmesan
- chopped parsley for garnish

Instructions

Using a sharp knife, slice potatoes into sections that are approximately an inch long.

Combine the potatoes, olive oil, Italian seasoning, garlic, salt, pepper, and Parmesan Cheese in a medium bowl.

Include in the air fryer's basket. Cook for 10 minutes at 400 degrees. Toss the potatoes into the basket and cook for a further 8 to 10 minutes, or until they are crisp and tender. Add chopped parsley as a garnish.

AIR-FRYER SWEET POTATO FRIES

Prep time: 5 minutes

Total time:20 minutes

Serving: 4

Ingredients

- 2 large sweet potatoes, cut into thin strips
- 2 tablespoons canola oil
- 1 teaspoon garlic powder
- 1 teaspoon paprika
- 1 teaspoon kosher salt
- 1/4 teaspoon cayenne pepper

Directions

the air fryer to 400 degrees. All ingredients should be combined and coated. In the air-fryer basket, place on a greased surface. Cook for 10–12 minutes, stirring once, until lightly browned. Serve right away.

AIR FRYER FROZEN VEGETABLES

Prep time: 1 minutes

Total time:16 minutes

Serving: 4

Ingredients

- 2 (10 oz) bags frozen mixed vegetables
- ½ teaspoon salt
- ½ teaspoon pepper
- 1 teaspoon garlic powder
- ½ teaspoon onion powder
- olive oil spray

Instructions

Add the frozen mixed veggies to the olive oil-sprayed air fryer basket. For optimal results, add frozen vegetables straight from the freezer to the air fryer without letting them thaw first.

Olive oil spray the tops of the veggies, then season with salt, pepper, garlic powder, and onion powder. Shake to combine.

For 10 minutes, cook in the air at 400 degrees. After shaking and stirring the vegetables, air fried them for an additional 5 to 10 minutes, or until crispy. In order to prevent burning, check frequently toward the conclusion of cooking depending on the air fryer model.

Add optional parmesan cheese before serving.

AIR FRYER BROCCOLI

Prep time: 5 minutes

Total time:15 minutes

Serving: 4

Ingredients

- Large florets from 2 broccoli crowns
- 3 tablespoons extra-virgin olive oil
- 1 tablespoon tamari
- ½ teaspoon garlic powder
- Red pepper flakes, optional for topping
- Sesame seeds, optional for topping

Instructions

Set the air fryer to 350°F for frying.

Combine the olive oil, tamari, and garlic powder with the broccoli in a big bowl. To prevent burning before the stalks are delicate, thoroughly coat the tops of the florets with your hands.

With a small gap between each floret, put the broccoli in a single coating in the air fryer basket. Work in groups if required.

Until delicate and golden brown, air fried for 8 to 10 minutes, flipping halfway through. If preferred, top with sesame seeds or red pepper flakes and serve hot.

BUFFALO CAULIFLOWER WITH BLUE CHEESE SAUCE

Prep time: 15 minutes

Total time:1 hours 20 minutes

Serving: 4

Ingredients

CHEESE SAUCE:

- 1/3 cup nonfat sour cream
- 2 tablespoons crumbled blue cheese
- 1 tablespoon skim milk
- 2 teaspoons mayonnaise
- Kosher salt and freshly ground black pepper

BUFFALO CAULIFLOWER:

- 2 tablespoons unsalted butter
- 1/4 cup hot sauce, such as Frank's
- 1 tablespoon freshly squeezed lemon juice
- 2 tablespoons olive oil
- Kosher salt
- 8 cups cauliflower florets

Directions

Set the oven to 400 degrees Fahrenheit.

The cheese sauce is: In a small bowl, mix the mayonnaise, milk, blue cheese, sour cream, 1/8 teaspoon salt, and a few tasks of black pepper. For around 30 minutes, cover and chill the food in the fridge.

In relation to Buffalo cauliflower: In the meantime, heat the butter in a small microwave-safe bowl on high. Lemon juice and spicy sauce are whisked in thereafter.

In a big bowl, combine 1/2 cup water, 1/4 teaspoon salt, and olive oil. Add the cauliflower and stir to thoroughly coat. Spread the cauliflower out on a rimmed baking sheet and roast for 20 to 25 minutes, or until it just starts to color and become tender. Once more whisking the hot sauce mixture, drip it over the cauliflower and toss to coat. For an additional 5 to 7 minutes, roast the cauliflower until the sauce is bubbling and the edges are browned. With the cheese sauce, serve hot.

AIR FRYER HONEY GLAZED CARROTS

Prep time: 5 minutes

Total time:15 minutes

Serving: 4

Ingredients

- 1 tablespoon olive oil
- 8 ounces baby carrots
- 1 tablespoon honey
- 1 tablespoon brown sugar
- ¼ teaspoon salt
- ¼ teaspoon pepper

Instructions

Air fryer basket should be lightly brushed with olive oil.

Combine the honey, brown sugar, salt, and pepper in a medium bowl.

Add the carrots and cover with the honey mixture in the bowl.

Carrots should be cooked for 8 to 10 minutes in an air fryer basket at 400 degrees Fahrenheit.

AIR FRYER FRIED RICE

Prep time: 5 minutes

Total time:20 minutes

Serving: 4

Ingredients

- 3 c rice cooked and cold
- 1 c frozen vegetables I used carrot, corn, broccoli and edamame
- ⅓ c coconut aminos
- 1 T oil
- 2 eggs scrambled

Instructions

Place your cold rice in a big bowl and proceed to prepare your air fryer fried rice.

The frozen vegetables can then be added to the rice bowl.

Add the protein to the rice bowl at this time, if you're using an egg or another type.

You will next add the oil and coconut aminos to your bowl.

Mix constantly until everything is mixed. The rice mixture should then be transferred to a baking-safe container.

That container should be put inside your air fryer. For 15 minutes, cook the air fryer fried rice at 360 degrees Fahrenheit. During the 15 minutes, I would advise stirring three times.

Enjoy!

DESSERT AND SNACKS RECIPES

AIR-FRYER CHOCOLATE CHIP OATMEAL COOKIES

Prep time: 20 minutes

Total time:30 minutes

Serving: 6

Ingredients

- 1 cup butter, softened
- 3/4 cup sugar
- 3/4 cup packed brown sugar
- 2 large eggs, room temperature
- 1 teaspoon vanilla extract
- 3 cups quick-cooking oats
- 1-1/2 cups all-purpose flour
- 1 package instant vanilla pudding mix
- 1 teaspoon baking soda
- 1 teaspoon salt
- 2 cups semisweet chocolate chips
- 1 cup chopped nuts

Directions

Set air fryer to 325 degrees. Cream the butter and sugars in a big bowl for 5-7 minutes, or until they are light and creamy. eggs and vanilla after mixing. Oats, flour, dry pudding mix, baking soda, and salt should all be whisked together before being gradually added to the creamed mixture. Add nuts and chocolate chips and stir.

By tablespoonfuls, drop the dough onto the baking sheets and gently press it down. Place in batches on oiled tray in air fryer basket, spacing 1 in. apart. Cook for 8 to 10 minutes. Remove and cool on wire racks.

AIR FRYER-BANANA BREAD

Prep time: 10 minutes

Total time:30 minutes

Serving: 6

Ingredients

- 1 1/3 cups of flour
- 1/2 cups of milk
- 1 teaspoon of baking powder
- 1 teaspoon of baking soda
- 1 teaspoon of cinnamon
- 1 teaspoon of salt
- 2/3 cups of sugar
- 1/2 cup of oil
- 3 overripe bananas

Instructions

In a mixer or a big mixing bowl, combine each item.

After that, apply nonstick cooking spray to coat your pan

Cook for 20 to 30 minutes at 330 degrees Fahrenheit in the air fryer. Does the toothpick come out clean when you check your air fryer? If so, it is finished; if not, let yourself a few more minutes.

Slice after cooling, then plate.

AIR-FRYER MINI NUTELLA DOUGHNUT HOLES

Prep time: 30 minutes

Total time:40 minutes

Serving: 32

Ingredients

- 1 large egg
- 1 tablespoon water
- 1 tube (16.3 ounces) large refrigerated flaky biscuits
- 2/3 cup Nutella
- Confectioners' sugar

Directions

Set air fryer to 300 degrees. With water, whisk the egg. Roll each biscuit into a 6-in. circle on a lightly dusted surface, then cut each into four wedges. Brush each wedge lightly with the egg mixture and then top with a spoonful of Nutella. Bring the edges up over the filling and firmly pinch them shut.

Wedge arrangements should be made in batches on an ungreased tray in the air-fryer basket. Cook for 8 to 10 minutes, flipping once, until golden brown. Serve warm and sprinkle with confectioners' sugar.

AIR FRYER PEANUT BUTTER COOKIES

Prep time: 5 minutes

Total time:10 minutes

Serving: 24

Ingredients

- 1 cup peanut butter creamy
- 1 cup granulated white sugar
- 1 egg

Instructions

In a medium-sized mixing bowl, combine the sugar, egg, and peanut butter.

Put some parchment paper in the Air Fryer basket's base.

Scoop the cookie batter onto the parchment paper using a 1 inch cookie scoop. Make mash marks with a fork.

Place the basket inside the Air Fryer, and cook for 4–5 minutes at 400°F.

The cookies should chill for a rare minutes in the Air Fryer basket before being taken out and put on a cooling rack.

AIR FRYER CHERRY TURNOVERS

Prep time: 10 minutes

Total time:30 minutes

Serving: 8

Ingredients

CHERRY TURNOVERS

- 1 Box 1 Pound puff pastry sheets, 1 large or 2 small sheets
- 1 Cup cherry pie filling
- 1 Large egg
- 2 tsps water

ICING DRIZZLE

- ½ Cup powdered sugar
- 1 Tbsps milk or cream

Instructions

CHERRY TURNOVERS

The egg and water should be lightly beaten in a small bowl before being placed aside.

The thawed puff pastry sheet should be unrolled and cut into eight rectangles. My 8-piece, 1-pound sheet measured roughly 15 by 13 inches; other sheets are just half this size.

Each rectangle should have about 2 teaspoons of filling on one end.

Around the filling, egg wash the pastry's three borders.

With a fork, close the edges of the rectangle's other end by folding it over the filling. With the fork, make a few holes in the top of each turnover. Egg wash should be applied to the turnovers' tops.

Leave a slight gap between each turnover as you place it in the basket.

For 17 minutes, set the air fryer to 320°F. Turnovers are considered to be finished when their shells are puffy, golden, and crisp. Put them about in the air fryer for 1-2 minutes if they aren't near ruined.

Turnovers that have baked should be taken out of the fryer and placed on a cooling rack. If you couldn't fit them all in your fryer, continue with the second batch of baking.

Drizzle icing over the turnovers once they have cooled, then serve.

ICING DRIZZLE

Mix the milk or cream and granulated sugar in a little bowl until the sugar dissolves and the icing is smooth and pourable.

AIR FRYER CHOCOLATE DOUGHNUTS

Prep time: 15 minutes

Total time:2 hours 30 minutes

Serving: 6

Ingredients

DOUGHNUTS

- ½ cup whole milk warmed to 100-110°F
- ½ cup granulated sugar
- 2¼ teaspoons active dry yeast 1 packet
- 3 tablespoons salted butter melted
- 1 large egg
- 1 teaspoon pure vanilla extract
- 1¾ cups all-purpose flour
- ¼ cup unsweetened cocoa powder

ICING

- 1 cup + 2 tablespoons powdered sugar
- 2 tablespoons unsweetened cocoa powder
- ¼ cup heavy cream
- Sprinkles, nuts, or oreo crumbs optional topping

Instructions

DOUGHNUTS

Mix the yeast, milk, and 2 tablespoons of sugar in a sizable basin. Give the mixture five minutes to rest, or until the yeast starts to foam. I advise throwing it away and beginning over if it doesn't foam and smell strongly of yeast.

Combine the remaining sugar, melted butter, egg, and vanilla before adding. A standard whisk would work at this point if you don't have a danish dough whisk, which is my preferred instrument for preparing doughs.

Add the cocoa powder and flour next. Just enough to blend.

The dough should form a soft, slightly tacky dough after 2 to 3 minutes of gentle kneading on a floured surface.

Once the dough has almost doubled in size, about an hour, transfer it to a bowl that has been lightly greased and lay it somewhere warm to rise.

Depending on how thick you want your doughnuts to be, roll out the dough on a lightly dusted surface to a thickness of between 14 and 2 inches.

To make doughnuts out of the dough, use a circular cookie cutter. To cut out my doughnuts, I used a 2.5" cookie cutter and a piping tip with a big aperture.

The doughnuts should be placed on a sheet pan and let to rise for an additional hour in a warm location.

Transfer four to six doughnuts carefully to the air fryer basket. Cook the doughnuts for 7 to 8 minutes at 300°F, or until they are soft inside and slightly crunchy outside. Before icing, move the doughnuts to a wire rack to finish cooling.

ICING

In a small bowl, mix the cocoa powder and powdered sugar.

I prefer a fairly thick frosting, so add the heavy cream gradually while whisking (about the consistency of pudding).

After the doughnuts have cooled, dip them in frosting and decorate them with sprinkles, nuts, oreos, or even flaky sea salt. Serve right away.

Doughnuts can be kept at room temperature in an airtight receptacle for up to two daytimes.

AIR FRYER BISCUITS (CANNED + REFRIGERATED)

Prep time: 10 minutes

Total time:10 minutes

Serving: 4

Ingredients

- 1 Refrigerated Can of Flaky Biscuits

Instructions

Take the biscuits out of the refrigerator. In the air fryer, put the biscuits.

For 9–10 minutes, air fry biscuits at 330°F/165°C. After cooking for about halfway, turn the biscuits over. (Make sure to check the biscuits in the waning minutes to see if the cook time has to be adjusted.)

Remove the biscuits with care, then serve them with gravy or jam. Enjoy!

EASY AIR FRYER BROWNIES

Prep time: 5 minutes

Total time:20 minutes

Serving: 4

Ingredients

- ½ cup all-purpose flour
- 6 Tablespoon unsweetened cocoa powder
- ¾ cup sugar
- ¼ cup unsalted butter melted
- 2 large eggs
- 1 Tablespoon vegetable oil
- ½ teaspoon vanilla extract
- ¼ teaspoon salt
- ¼ teaspoon baking powder

Instructions

Butter the bottom and the sides of your 7-inch baking pan liberally to prepare it. Place aside.

Set your air fryer to 330 degrees Fahrenheit and let it run for about 5 minutes while you are mixing the brownie batter.

Put the all-purpose flour, sugar, butter, eggs, oil, vanilla extract, salt, and baking powder into a large bowl. Stir to mix everything together.

It should be added and the top smoothed out in the baking pan.

Bake for 15 minutes in your preheated Air Fryer, or until a toothpick inserted in the center comes out largely clean.

Before removing and cutting, remove from the pan and let cool.

AIR FRYER LAVA CAKES

Prep time: 5 minutes

Total time: 25 minutes

Serving: 2

Ingredients

- ⅓ cup semisweet chocolate chips
- ¼ cup unsalted butter
- ½ cup powdered sugar
- 1 large egg
- 1 large egg yolk
- ½ teaspoon vanilla extract
- ⅛ teaspoon salt
- 3 tablespoons all-purpose flour

Directions

Achieve a 350°F air fryer temperature (175 degrees C). Grease two separate ramekins.

In a bowl that can be microwaved, mix butter and chocolate chips. One minute on high in the microwave. Stir and heat for approximately 15 seconds in the microwave. Once the chocolate is all melted and blended, remove from the microwave and stir.

Melt the chocolate and whisk in the powdered sugar, egg, egg yolk, vanilla essence, and salt. Flour should be added and combined thoroughly. Put the prepared ramekins in the air fryer basket after pouring the batter into them. Large sheets of foil should be used to cover the ramekins; the edges should be tucked under to prevent foil from flying off.

For 8 to 10 minutes, cook. After removing the foil, cook for an additional 2 to 4 minutes, or until the edges are firm. Take out of the air fryer, then stand aside for five minutes.

Serve right away after inverting onto dessert plates.

KOREAN FRIED CHICKEN

Prep time: 15 minutes

Total time:30 minutes

Serving: 4

Ingredients

FOR THE CHICKEN

- 500g chicken wings
- large chunk of ginger, finely grated
- 50g cornflour
- vegetable oil, for frying
- sesame seeds and sliced spring onion, to serve

FOR THE SAUCE

- 6 tbsp dark brown sugar
- 2 tbsp gochujang
- 2 tbsp soy sauce
- 2 large garlic cloves, crushed
- small piece ginger, grated
- 2 tsp sesame oil

Directions

Put all the ingredients in a pot and gently simmer for 3–4 minutes, or until the sauce is syrupy. Remove from the heat and leave aside.

Grated ginger, salt, and pepper are used to season the chicken wings. Cornflour the chicken and toss to coat well.

A big frying pan with around 2 cm of vegetable oil in it should be heated on medium-high. Chicken wings should be fried for 8 to 10 minutes, flipping them halfway through. Remove from the oil and set on some paper towels. Allow to gently cool (around 2 mins).

Place the chicken wings in the sauce after it has been reheated. Place in a bowl and garnish with spring onion slices and sesame seeds.

TANDOORI CHICKEN

Prep time: 6 hours

Total time:6 hours 20 minutes

Serving: 4

Ingredients

- 2 lbs chicken drumsticks skim removed
- ½ cup plain regular or low fat yogurt
- 1 tablespoon garlic paste
- 1 tablespoon ginger paste
- 1 tablespoon lemon juice
- 1 to 2 tablespoons kashmiri or any other mild red chili powder
- ½ teaspoon ground turmeric
- 1 to 2 teaspoons garam masala
- 2 teaspoons kosher salt
- 1 tablespoon oil

TO SERVE

- 1 lime cut in wedges
- 1 small red onion sliced

Instructions

each drumstick with 3–4 slits. The marinade is made by combining yogurt, ginger, garlic, lemon juice, red chili powder, turmeric, garam masala, and salt. Apply evenly to the chicken pieces and marinate for at least 5 to 6 hours or up to 24 hours in the refrigerator.

Set the oven or grill to 450 degrees. 30 minutes before cooking, remove the chicken from the fridge. Place the chicken on a grill pan or outdoor barbecue after baste-ing it with some cooking oil.

It can be grilled outside for 20 minutes or until the juices are clear. Alternatively, bake it for 15 minutes in the oven, then broil it for 5 minutes to achieve some perfectly seared grill marks.

Serve with thinly sliced red onion and fresh lime wedges.

CHICKEN JALFREZI

Prep time: 20 minutes

Total time:1 hours 15 minutes

Serving: 6

Ingredients

- 2 tablespoons vegetable oil
- 1 onion, grated
- 2 cloves garlic, chopped
- 1 ½ pounds boneless skinless chicken thighs, cut in half
- 3 teaspoons ground turmeric
- 1 teaspoon chili powder
- 1 ½ teaspoons salt
- can peeled and diced tomatoes
- tablespoons ghee
- teaspoons ground cumin
- teaspoons ground coriander
- 2 tablespoons grated fresh ginger root
- ½ cup chopped cilantro leaves

Directions

In a sizable deep skillet, heat the oil over medium-high heat. Cook the onions and garlic for around two minutes. Salt, turmeric, and chili powder are used to season the chicken after adding it. Gently fry the chicken, flipping it periodically and scraping the bottom of the pan.

Add the tomatoes and their juice, cover the pan, and simmer for 20 minutes over medium heat. After 10 minutes of simmering without the cover, the extra liquid will have evaporated.

For an additional 5 to 7 minutes, add the ghee, cumin, ginger, cilantro, and ground coriander. Sauce should be spooned on top of the chicken pieces before serving.

MUSHROOM TURKEY BURGER

Prep time: 55 minutes

Total time:2 hours 55 minutes

Serving: 4

Ingredients

- 2 tablespoons extra-virgin olive oil, plus more for brushing the grill grates
- 2 cups cremini mushrooms, finely chopped
- 1/4 cup finely chopped shallots
- 2 garlic cloves, chopped
- 1 1/4 pounds ground turkey
- 1/2 cup Greek yogurt, plus extra for the buns
- 1/2 cup dry breadcrumbs
- 1 large egg, beaten
- Kosher salt and freshly ground black pepper
- 4 brioche buns, split and toasted
- 4 slices ripe tomato
- 16 thin cucumber slices

Directions

Over medium-high heat, add the oil to a medium skillet. When the oil is burning, add the mushrooms and sauté for 2 to 3 minutes, turning them once, until the bottoms are browned. After about 2 minutes of stirring and browning on the opposite side, reduce the heat to medium and add the shallots and garlic. About 5 minutes of cooking and stirring is required to soften the shallots. Cool the mixture after turning off the heat.

In a sizable bowl, combine the turkey, yogurt, breadcrumbs, egg, and cooled mushrooms. Add salt and pepper to taste. Don't overmix; just gently stir the ingredients together with a wooden spoon to blend. Four 1-inch-thick patties should be formed. Refrigerate for up to a day (two to three hours).

Grill or grill pan should be heated to medium-high. The patties' exteriors should be salted and peppered. Oil the grill grates and then grill the burgers for about 6 minutes per side, or until they are well-marked, cooked through, and the inner temperature gets 155 to 160 phases F. Slices of tomato, cucumber, and added yogurt should be placed on the buns.

CRISPY CHICKEN TENDERS

Prep time: 10 minutes

Total time:30 minutes

Serving: 4

Ingredients

- 1 large egg
- 2 tablespoons olive oil
- 2 tablespoons lemon juice
- 1 tablespoon fresh chopped parsley
- 2 teaspoons minced garlic
- 3/4 teaspoon salt to season
- 1/4 teaspoon cracked black pepper
- 28 ounces (800 g) chicken tenders
- 1 cup Panko breadcrumbs
- 1/2 cup regular breadcrumbs
- 1 teaspoon mild paprika
- 1/2 teaspoon garlic powder
- 1/2 teaspoon onion powder
- 1/4 cup fresh grated parmesan cheese

Instructions

Oven should be heated to 400°F (200°C). Grease a baking sheet or pan with a thin layer of oil or cooking oil spray. Place aside.

Mix the egg, oil, lemon juice, parsley, garlic, salt, and pepper in a big bowl.

While preparing the crumb mixture, dip the chicken tenders in the egg mixture and let them sit for 5 minutes.

OPTIONAL: For 30 to 60 minutes, marinate in the refrigerator under cover.

Both types of breadcrumbs, paprika, garlic powder, onion powder, and parmesan cheese should be combined in a separate bowl.

In order to coat the chicken uniformly, dredge it in the breadcrumb/parmesan mixture.

Place the tenders there and mist the surface with cooking oil spray.

For ten minutes, bake. Turn over and bake for an additional 5 to 10 minutes, or until well done.

AIR FRYER CHICKEN NUGGETS

Prep time: 10 minutes

Total time:25 minutes

Serving: 4

Ingredients

- 1 lb. boneless chicken cut into strips or 2×2 size.
- 1 cup flour divided in half
- ½ cup milk
- 1 tsp salt
- ½ tsp pepper
- ½ tsp paprika
- 1 cup bread crumbs
- 2 Tablespoons olive oil

Instructions

FOR THE BREADCRUMBS

You can manufacture your own bread crumbs from roughly four slices of bread, depending on the size of the loaf. Place the bread in the basket and set the oven to 350 degrees for around 5-7 minutes, flipping the bread over halfway through. The bread gets really crisp with the air fryer! After placing my bread in the food processor, I had excellent, brand-new bread crumbs in just a few short seconds.

FOR THE CHICKEN NUGGETS:

Oil should be applied to the basket using a pastry brush in order to prepare it. (I used olive oil, but vegetable oil would also work.) By doing this, you can prevent the batter from adhering to the cooking basket.) Discard the basket.

Whisk together the remaining 1/2 cup flour, milk, and seasonings in a small to medium bowl. Place two other bowls next to each other for convenient dipping, one containing the remaining 1/2 cup flour and the other the breadcrumbs. Per piece of chicken should be dropped in flour first, then into a mixture of milk and seasonings, and last into bread crumbs. Without piling, put each piece into the oiled basket. Once all the pieces are coated and in the basket, repeat coating each one.

Make sure the chicken is chicken and that it is 380 degrees. Cook for 7 minutes on each side. Cook for an extra minute on each side if you prefer your food extra crispy.

Serve right away.

BACON WRAPPED CHICKEN THIGHS

Prep time: 10 minutes

Total time:25 minutes

Serving: 4

Ingredients

- 8 boneless skinless chicken thighs ~ 4-ounces each
- kosher salt to taste
- freshly ground black pepper to taste
- 8 bacon slices ideally thin slices

Instructions

Set the oven to 400°F.

Place a baking sheet with a rim covered in foil within an oven-safe rack. Chicken thighs should be salted and peppered with kosher salt. Place each chicken thigh on the rack of the baking sheet after being wrapped in a slice of bacon (keeping the thighs as flat as possible and taking care to minimize how much the bacon strip overlaps itself). Bake for 25 to 30 minutes.

BUFFALO CHICKEN WING SAUCE

Prep time: 5 minutes

Total time: 5 minutes

Serving: 8

Ingredients

- ⅔ cup hot pepper sauce
- ½ cup cold unsalted butter
- 1 ½ tablespoons white vinegar
- ¼ teaspoon Worcestershire sauce
- ¼ teaspoon cayenne pepper
- ⅛ teaspoon garlic powder
- salt to taste

Directions

In a pot over medium heat, combine hot sauce, butter, vinegar, Worcestershire sauce, cayenne, garlic powder, and salt. Stirring with a whisk, bring to a simmer. Remove the saucepan from the heat as soon as the liquid starts to bubble up the sides, whisk the mixture, and then reserve for use.

Printed in Great Britain
by Amazon

33164024R00059